MICHELANGELO'S *DAVID*

HANDLE WITH CARE

FIRENZE
MVSEI

For further in-depth information on the topics dealt with herein, see *L'Accademia, Michelangelo, l'Ottocento*, edited by Franca Falletti, in the study series on the Galleria dell'Accademia "The Place for David".

ISBN 88-8347-126-1

© 2002 Ministero per i Beni e le Attività Culturali
Soprintendenza Speciale per il Patrimonio Storico, Artistico ed Etnoantropologico e per il Polo Museale della città di Firenze
Second reprint: July 2009

A publication by
s i l l a b e
Livorno
www.sillabe.it

managing editor: *Maddalena Paola Winspeare*
graphic design: *Susanna Coseschi*
translation: *Anthony Cafazzo*
editing: *Giulia Bastianelli*

reproduction rights: *archivio Sillabe: Paolo Nannoni, Remo Bardazzi, Nicolò Orsi Battaglini, Sara Zinelli;*
Rabatti & Domingie; Archivio Gabinetto fotografico della Soprintendenza per il Polo Museale Fiorentino;
Archivio Museo di Casa Buonarroti

photolithography: *La Nuova Lito* - Firenze

The publisher is at the disposal of the copyright holders of images from unidentified sources.

Franca Falletti

DAVID

MICHELANGELO'S *DAVID*

sillabe

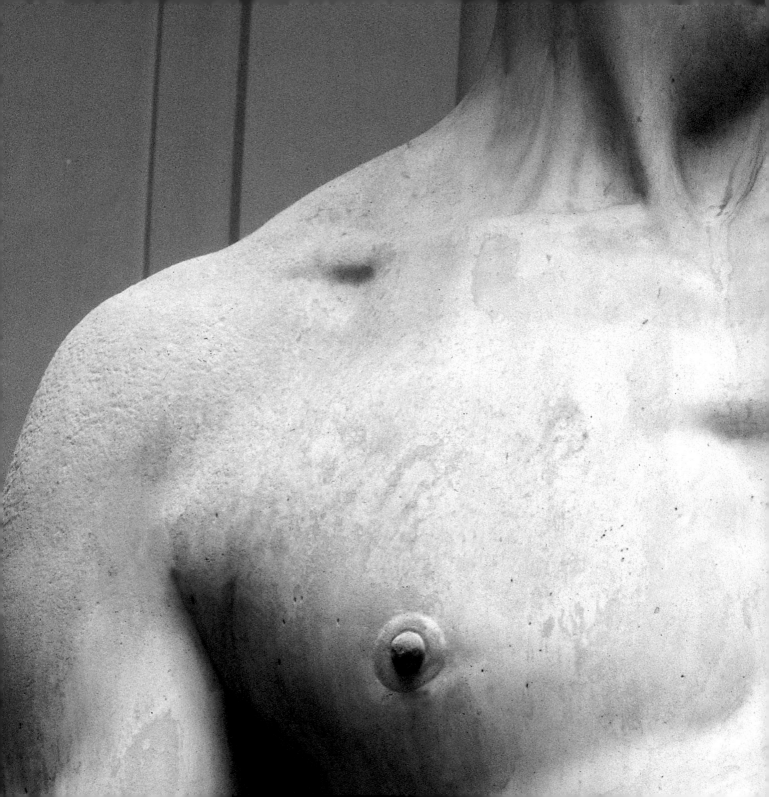

Contents

A brief biography of Michelangelo 7

Michelangelo's *David* 13

An itinerary through Michelangelo's works in Florence 61

A brief biography of Michelangelo

Michelangelo was born to Ludovico Buonarroti and Francesca di Neri del Serra in the town of Caprese, near Arezzo. His family, originally from Florence, was living in Caprese because his father had been named *podestà* (head magistrate of the town). At the end of his term of office, the family returned to Florence. As was the custom of the time, as a child Michelangelo was given over to the care of a nanny, the wife of a stonemason from Settignano. He therefore grew up in the midst of stone and marble.

At age twelve he was sent to study at the workshop of painters Domenico and David del Ghirlandaio, at the time one of the busiest and well-organised ateliers in Florence, on a par with Botticelli's. It was however certainly not one of the most innovative, and this fact, together with the preference Michelangelo showed for sculpture, makes it easy to imagine how he would wish to leave such a restricted environment as soon as possible. So, in 1490 he abandoned the shop, was taken in by Lorenzo il Magnifico and began his frequent, impassioned visits to the Gardens of San Marco, where amongst the wide-ranging art collections of the Medici, artists studied under the guidance of Bertoldo di Giovanni. Most importantly, here they were able to interact and exchange ideas with highly cultured humanists and men of letters such as Marsilio Ficino and Pico della Mirandola, thereby giving rise to a learned Academy *ante litteram*. From those years spent in the ambience of the Medici come Michelangelo's first documented works, the *Madonna of the Stairs, Battle of the Centaurs* (Florence, Casa Buonarroti) and the *Wooden Crucifix* at Santo Spirito.

This period, certainly one of the most significant in the young sculptor's formation, was however suddenly interrupted by the tragic events that overwhelmed Florence during the last years of the century: the death of Lorenzo il Magnifico, the invasion of King Charles VIII and the bloody episode of Fra' Savonarola. The need to find other life and work opportunities outside Florence drove Michelangelo first to Venice and Bologna, where he worked on completing the Arca (Shrine) di San Domenico, and finally Rome, where he resided from 1496 to

Opposite:
Madonna of the Stairs, ca 1490, Florence, Casa Buonarroti Museum

Battle of the Centaurs, 1490-1492, Florence, Casa Buonarroti Museum

1501 under the care and protection of the banker Jacopo Galli. A curious episode leads to his success in Rome: with the help of Lorenzo di Pierfrancesco de' Medici, Michelangelo places a marble *Sleeping Cupid* on the market, passing it off as a Roman artefact. Cardinal Raffaele Riario purchased it, and after discovering the deception, wanted to meet the author of so skilful an imitation. Thus, Michelangelo was called to the papal court and commissioned with *Bacchus,* today in the Bargello National Museum in Florence. During this first Roman period he also carried out the *Pietà* in the Vatican Basilica of St. Peter, as well as the two panels, the *Risen Christ* and the *Manchester Madonna,* now in the National Gallery, London.

 In 1501 Michelangelo returned to Florence, where he remained until 1505, the period during which he worked on *David*. At the same time he also executed a series of exceptionally celebrated and demanding works: four of the twelve *Apostles* for the Piccolomini altar in the Siena Cathedral and *St. Matthew* for the Florence Cathedral, today in the Gallery of the Accademia. He moreover performed a *Bronze David*, now lost, a *Madonna and Child* for the Cathedral in Bruges, the *Taddei Tondo* (London, Royal Academy), the *Pitti Tondo* (Florence, Bargello), the *Doni Tondo* (Florence, Uffizi) and some cartoons for the fresco of the Battle of Cascina for the Salone dei Cinquecento (Hall of the Five hundred)

Crucifix, 1492-1493, Florence, Church of Santo Spirito

Francesco Granacci, *Charles VIII's entry into Florence*, 1518-1527, Florence, Uffizi, Storehouse

Following page:
Saint Matthew, 1505-1506, Florence, Gallery of the Accademia

Bacchus, 1496-1497, Florence, Bargello National Museum

in Palazzo Vecchio. We can only guess at the superhuman physical resistance and inexhaustible creativity with which Michelangelo must have been gifted to enable him to produce so much, with such consistent, extraordinary quality, moreover almost always executing it himself, or in any event never availing himself of a true workshop of his own. Returning once again to Rome, he was commissioned by Pope Julius II della Rovere to design and carry out his sepulchral monument, originally planned as a imposing work to be placed in the centre of St. Peter's Basilica. The commission, for which Michelangelo justifiably had such great expectations, instead became his life's torment because of the constant reductions in its scope. In 1542 the final work, modified beyond recognition from his original idea,

was placed in San Pietro in Vincoli, in the form it can still be viewed today, with *Moses* in its centre.

However, despite the many struggles and disappointments, beginning in 1508 Michelangelo lived and worked primarily in Rome, with more or less brief sojourns in his native Florence, connected for the most part to his work on the monument complex of San Lorenzo: completion of the basilica's façade, the *Medici Tombs* in the New Sacristy and the library. During the siege of Florence by the troops of Charles v in 1530, he also took part in planning the city's defences. When in Florence Michelangelo often travelled to the quarries in the Apuan Alps to choose his own marbles, marking his selections with three intersecting circles, within which the initials of the quarryman would be added. Each job that he accepted therefore required direct personal involvement far greater than other artists of his time.

In the papal city, on the other hand, most of his time was spent on the extraordinary undertakings of painting the Sistine and Paolina Chapels, as well as the architectural and urban planning of the Capitol,

St. Peter's, Palazzo Farnese and many of the city's most important civil and religious buildings. In the middle and late periods of his life, Michelangelo did not actually do much sculpturing, some of the most noteworthy works being the *Risen Christ* for Santa Maria sopra Minerva, completed in 1521, and the bust of *Brutus,* commissioned from him by the émigré Florentine Niccolò Ridolfi in about 1540.

In Rome, which he would never leave from 1534 until his death in 1564, Michelangelo established deep bonds of friendship with some exponents of the Protestant Reformation, in particular the poet, Vittoria Colonna, with whom he shared a need for renewed spirituality and a passion for poetry. In fact, Michelangelo himself wrote verse and had even arranged to publish them, an enterprise quashed by the premature death of his inspiring muse in 1547. Nevertheless, a rich collection of his verses has survived in manuscript form and provides us with great insight into the heart and mind of this genius.

It appears to be Michelangelo's contact with Vittoria Colonna

and her circle of friends that was also responsible for his return to sculpture and, especially, the theme of the *Pietà,* which he tackles twice in the twilight of his life: the sculptural group initially designed for his own tomb and now in the Museo dell'Opera del Duomo (Cathedral Works Museum) in Florence, and the *Rondanini Pietà,* to which he dedicated himself until his death, ever restless, ever unsatisfied with that which issued from his hands.

Michelangelo's *David*

In the beginning: a challenge

In many respects the story of Michelangelo's *David* is an unusual one. As already mentioned, the sculptor generally devoted great care to the choice of materials on which he was to work. He would travel in person to the heart of the Apuan Alps to select the marble blocks that best suited his needs, dealing directly with the quarrymen and following all stages of excavation and transportation.

This was not the case for *David*: Michelangelo found the block ready to be sculpted. In fact, it had even been partly worked by other artists before him: Agostino di Duccio, who had put his hand to it in 1464, and then Bernardo Rossellino in 1476. We do not know exactly what condition the marble was in when it passed into Michelangelo's hands, but there is no doubt that sculpting it involved particular difficulties, as the enterprise had been abandoned twice before. The piece was in fact not onlyhuge, but marred by numerous veins (especially in what are now the legs), whose presence greatly increased the risk of sudden cracking.

However, Michelangelo was young, and the commission prestigious. What is more, the challenge to man's power to overcome material adversities must certainly have enticed the sculptor's tenacious and combative nature. Thus, fittingly, *David*, vanquisher of the dread Goliath, hero of the impossible challenge, was apparently born of an equally impossible challenge.

The sculpting of David
and its placement in Piazza della Signoria

David was originally commissioned from Michelangelo in 1501 by the Opera del Duomo (the Cathedral Works' Authority) to adorn one of the buttresses on the apse section of the Florentine Cathedral, Santa Maria del Fiore. However, when the work was concluded in 1504, its destination was changed: Pier Soderini, the supreme gonfalonier of justice of the Florentine Republic, wanted it placed near Palazzo Vecchio, that is, the seat of the city's political and civil power. It is unknown what exactly prompted this change of heart, but those were years in which the Florentines had seen the definitive loss of their republic, and the city was

Florence, Palazzo Vecchio, 13th century

Florence, Palazzo Vecchio, inner courtyard

fraught with poisonous tensions and shaken by dramatic events. Thus, artists and their works were often called on to play crucial roles as symbols of one party or the other in the never-ending struggle for power.

The decision of exactly where to put the *David* was made on January 25th, 1504. The reasons were set forth in a report by the committee of artists expressly chosen to decide, which included such esteemed and well-known personages as Andrea della Robbia, Piero di Cosimo, Pietro Perugino, Leonardo da Vinci, Filippino Lippi, Sandro Botticelli and Cosimo Rosselli. As testified to by written accounts of the heated debates that took place during the committee meetings, many of its members (in particular a group headed by Giuliano da Sangallo) harboured strong hostile feelings towards the emerging young sculptor and tried to avoid a position of inordinate prestige, such as that which Michelangelo was hoping for – at the entrance to Palazzo Vecchio. Various alternative proposals were made, amongst which, the inner courtyard of the same building or the Loggia dei Lanzi just outside. The presence of contrasting factions and the growing tension with regard to artistic choices, which inevitably also took on political

overtones, mixed with personal rancour and jealousy, eventually incited a number of turbulent incidents when the sculpture was transported from the courtyard of the Opera del Duomo, where it had been sculpted, to the spot where it had been ordained to stand – in Piazza della Signoria. The move was made between May 14th and 18th, 1504, and has been described in some memoirs of the time[1]: "The 14th day of May MDIV, the marble Colossus was carried out of the workshop, it came forth at 24:00 hours, and they broke the wall above the door so that it could pass, and on that night stones were hurled at the Colossus to damage it; it had to be guarded during the night and moved very slowly and bound so upright, with sturdy planks and great ingenuity, so it was suspended and did not touch ground with its feet, and it laboured four days to come to the square: it arrived in the square at 12:00 hours of the 18th day, it called for more than 40 men to move it, beneath were four greased trunks, and these were passed from hand to hand and they struggled until the 8th day of June, 1504 to place it within the railing where Judith stood, which had to be removed…"

Some paintings depicting Piazza della Signoria before 1504 show Donatello's *Judith and Holofernes* (the Judith in the document just cited) still in place, where it would be replaced by the "Colossus", as the Florentines immediately rechristened the new statue. On June 11th, Cronaca and Antonio da Sangallo were commissioned to create a special pedestal, and Michelangelo worked the entire summer to finish his work, which was unveiled to the Florentine people on the following September 8th.

Right from the first moments of its existence, therefore, *David* is the focal point of contrasts, struggles and violent controversy, and prompts heated debate over its placement: a curious destiny as catalyst of the city's discontent that would accompany it forever.

Late 15th-century Florentine painter, *Martyrdom of Savonarola in Piazza della Signoria*, ca 1498, Florence, Museum of San Marco

But where shall we put this David?

Further doubts and debates over where to put *David* resurfaced in the early 19th century, prompted, in particular, by the wide-spread interest focused on Piazza della Signoria as a site representative of the Florentine values of secular republican liberty – values befitting the particular political climate accompanying the early spread of the Risorgimento and the emergence of a new awareness of the city's place in history.

Human carelessness and misguided restoration operations had caused the sculpture's state of preservation to quickly deteriorate. Already before the 1840s, the need was being felt to move the masterpiece to a more sheltered setting to protect it from the elements and damage consequent to wagon traffic and atmospheric pollution. The first to advance a concrete proposal was the sculptor and professor Lorenzo Bartolini, who on June 15th, 1842 in a letter to Girolamo Ballati Nerli, director of the Scrittoio delle Fortezze e Fabbriche (Office of Fortresses and Workshops), sounded the alarm and called for the prompt safeguarding of *David* in a more secure area, the Loggia dei Lanzi, according to a project by the architect Pasquale Poccianti[2]. Despite this, and despite the evident worsening of the statue's conditions, it was only ten years later, in 1852, that a commission was named to study the effective state of the statue and decide upon its future. The chosen place obviously had to offer protection from dangers of all sorts, but it also had to do justice to the statue's stunning perfection with appropriate lighting and suitably spacious surroundings. Two further essential conditions were that the site be worthy of the work's status and, at the same time, that it allow it to be viewed by all the citizenry.

Pasquale Poccianti, *The Loggia dei Lanzi with Michelangelo's David in the centre*, ASF (Florence State Archives), *Annex of the Segreteria di Gabinetto*, file 121, drawing attached to insert 18

17

Florence, View of the Uffizi Gallery, 1560

Pietro and Ferdinando Tacca, *Monument to Ferdinando I*, 17th century, Florence, Museum of the Medici Chapels, Chapel of Princes

No unequivocal decision was however reached, though the commission did narrow the field to three possible solutions: the Loggia dei Lanzi, the Loggia del Mercato Vecchio (i.e., the Old Market) and the wide archway at the end of the Uffizi arcade. The idea of the Old Market loggia was abandoned immediately because of the unsuitability of the filthy, foul-smelling surroundings, populated by traffickers and the indigent. The position under the Uffizi arcade also had numerous and well-motivated opponents: David would in fact have been too far-removed from the heart of the city, relegated to the end of a long architectural perspective. But what rightly caused the greatest misgivings was the fact that the lighting would have come from behind the statue, from the River Arno, with the consequent effect of leaving the sculpture's anterior in the shadow, irremediably flattening its vigorous shaping. In short, viewed from Piazza della Signoria, *David* would have appeared as an enfeebled silhouette of itself. Meanwhile, an entirely new idea was in the making: David could be, rather, had to be placed in a completely closed setting. This opened up many as yet unthought-of possibilities: the Chapel of Princes in San Lorenzo or the room known as the "Sala del Colosso di Montecavallo" in the Accademia di Belle Arti (the Fine Arts Academy).

It was in 1853 that for the first time a proposal was made, by Alessandro

Manetti, to design a site expressly for Michelangelo's masterpiece, *ex novo*³. Nevertheless, although opposed by many, the idea of the Loggia dei Lanzi made headway, and it was finally decided to test it out preliminarily by placing a plaster copy cast from a mould of the original made by Clemente Papi a few years prior. This replica stood in the loggia from July to October, 1854 and the decision of the experts was unanimously and emphatically negative.

Meanwhile, the years passed; *David* stayed put and, as one committee led to the next, one debate gave way to the next, its condition continued to worsen. One possibility that was considered was to build an iron and glass shelter around the statue, perhaps something similar to that enclosing the marble sculptural group by Lorenzo Bartolini in Piazza Demidoff, but it was thought that such a structure would be too intrusive and a blemish on the architectural harmony of the square and Palazzo Vecchio.

The unification of Italy and the establishment of its capital in Florence gave new vigour to the by now tiresome dissertations on David's future, and in 1866 the Ministry of Education called for a new experiment with the copy: the first floor hall of the National Museum of Bargello, amongst masterpieces of the Florentine Renaissance. The plaster remained there for about a year and a half, prompting conflicting reactions, until the idea was abandoned, above all thanks

Florence, The so-called room of the "Montecavallo Colossus" in the Gallery of the Accademia

Florence, Bargello National Museum, view of Donatello's Room

to Emilio De Fabris and his vision. In 1872, this architect, who had won the competition for the façade of Santa Maria del Fiore, managed to secure the commission for his design of an area devoted entirely to *David* inside the Accademia di Belle Arti. This is the turning point for creation of the Tribune and the beginning of the modern period in *David's* history.

On July 30th, 1873 the Colossus stirred for the second time, moving along the streets of Florence from Piazza della Signoria to arrive, after a trying seven-day journey, at the entranceway of the Accademia in Via del Cocomero (today Via Ricasoli), winding its way on a pair of railway tracks and sustained by a sort of wooden framework. On August 8th it was finally placed on its new pedestal, where it can still be admired today.

Transfer of Michelangelo's David from Piazza della Signoria to the Gallery of the Accademia di Belle Arti, from "Nuova Illustrazione Universale", anno I, n. 6, January 18 1874, p. 48

Following page:
Michelangelo's *David* being transported to the Accademia, Archive of the Florence Superintendency of Artistic and Historical Heritage

"In testimony to the relocation of Michelangelo Buonarroti's statue representing David from Palazzo della Signoria, where it was placed on the 11th day of June 1507, to the Accademia di Belle Arti, where it has stood upon a high pedestal since the 8th day of August, 1873.

On this day Wednesday, July 30th, 1873, antemeridian. Under the direction of the Mechanical Engineer Porra, the David (completely surrounded by a special scaffold and suspended) was removed from its raised base where the railing of Palazzo della Signoria once stood, and was lowered onto the rails that were to transport it to the Accademia di Belle Arti; it was then relocated in front of the post office, where Palazzo Lavison now stands.

On this day, Thursday, July 31st.

At the hour of 4 o'clock, antemeridian, the David was transported toward Via Calzajuolis by means of a platform on the rails leading into said road, stopping in front of the Buonajuti Bazaar, and thence to the lane once called Ru-

spanti, today *Coroncina*.
On this day, Friday, August 1st.
At the same hour, it was moved across the Cathedral square into Via Martelli, and left to rest in front of the block of Casamento degli Scolopi at St. Giovannino.
On this day, Saturday, August 2nd.
Hence it was moved, first to the square of the church of San Marco and then via the platform manoeuvred toward the Accademia di Belle Arti.
On this day, Sunday, August 3rd.
It has been moved once again, and therefore directed with a further manoeuvre of the platform to Via della Sapienza, up to the opening made for its introduction.
On this day, Monday, August 4th.
Once again at the same hour, from the street in whose midst it stood, it was turned again and introduced through the aforementioned opening into the hall between the street and the square, at 8 o'clock antemeridian.
On this day, Tuesday, August 5th.
It was drawn into the inner courtyard of the Accademia; and through two platform manoeuvres, brought before and in proximity of the new base on which it will henceforth have to stand, surrounded by a tribune or aedicule whose foundations have been readied after the design of Sir Prof. Architect De Fabris.
On this day, Wednesday, August 6th.
Turned once again, it was drawn towards the base, above which it was suspended in order to study the most suitable height for artistic effect.
Upon which Professors De Fabris, Porra, Pollastrini, Dupré and others were convened.
On this day Thursday, August 7th.
It has been retracted in order to reduce the height of the base by 63 (sixty-three) centimetres, because the previously prepared one was deemed too high.
On this day, Friday, August 8th.
It was brought back into place and lowered onto the base, where it is to stand as long as God wills. [...]"
(Florence, Archives of the Accademia di Belle Arti, file no. 62, year 1873, insert 30)

Saving David down through the ages

Michelangelo's *David* has not had an easy life even from the perspective of its preservation. As mentioned, the statue was sculpted from a piece of marble not chosen by Michelangelo, and despite its origins in the renowned Fantiscritti quarries overlooking Carrara (therefore from an area yielding undisputedly high-quality materials), right from the beginning it exhibited defects in veining and consistency. The veins in the block had already deterred Michelangelo's predecessors from undertaking such an exacting task under the continuous threat of cracking, and its consistency moreover made it appear "soft and baked" as Giuliano da Sangallo declared before the committee charged with deciding the stature's placement in January 1504[4]. It was for this reason that Sangallo and his faction argued against putting the Colossus out in the open, especially where it would be completely exposed, as within the railing of Palazzo Vecchio. However, as we have seen, it was decided otherwise, and the consequences soon made themselves known.

As Jacopo Nardi narrates[5], when in 1512 Pier Soderini, head of the Florentine Republic, was exiled from the city to allow re-entry of the Medici family, the indignation and wrath of the heavens manifested themselves through many signs, amongst which the thunderbolt that struck Palazzo Vecchio and then ricocheted against the plinth holding *David,* rocking it and seriously damaging it in the process. In effect, the pedestal's instability is underscored in a number of 19th-century documents, though it was also attributed in part to wagons bumping against the statue's base in the narrow section of the square.

Then, as if *David* were cursed by an especially ill fate, only a few years later, during the 1527 revolt set off by the banishing of the Medici from Florence, its left arm was fractured at the point where the hand holds the sling. Some rioters had

Opposite:
Model of the wagon used to transport *David* from Piazza della Signoria to the Gallery of the Accademia, 1873, Florence, Casa Buonarroti Museum

On this and following page:
Details of the marble surface of Michelangelo's *David*

Gamma-ray photography revealing the pins inserted to mend the breaks in the right arm.

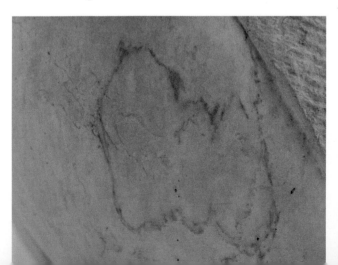

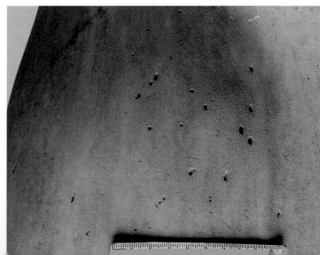

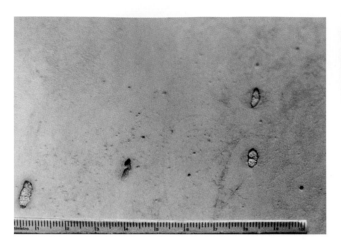

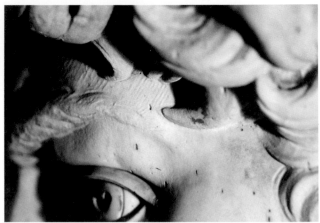

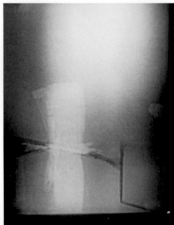

barricaded themselves inside Palazzo Vecchio to defend themselves, while others tried to break down the doors to the courtyard. Those inside started throwing all sorts of objects from the windows, until something accidentally struck the sculpture. In the general mayhem, the marble fragments were left lying on the ground in the square. It was only three days later that Giorgio Vasari and Cecchino Salviati, little more than children at the time, picked them up and brought them to Salviati's father, who preserved them. Finally, in 1543 he delivered them to Duke Cosimo I, who had them fixed back in place with some copper pins. Apparently, no one had found anything to complain about in the fact that *David* remained mutilated for sixteen years!

Little information is available on *David's* state of maintenance from the mid-16th century to the early 19th century, except that at some undetermined time it was continuously battered by a jet of rainwater pouring from a broken roof-gutter on the building. Once again, there was no sign of particularly prompt intervention, which confirms that at the time *David* was regarded as "just another statue", still far from taking on that mythical, almost sacred aura that surrounds it today.

The documental evidence resumes in 1813, when the sculptor Stefano Ricci presents an estimate of 45 gold sequins "… to restore, polish and encausticate the statue of *Davidde* by the Immortal Michelangelo"[6]. Applying encaustics was a technique once used in wall painting. It consisted of adding wax to plaster mortar and making the substances interact by heating. As no sources are available that expressly illustrate exactly how encaustics were used to protect sculptures, we can only imagine that it was a wax layer applied warm, mixed perhaps with other elements as well. In fact, oils and waxes are commonly used to protect stone surfaces. We do not even know whether *David,* before the restoration carried out by Ricci, had ever had some sort of finishing, or what it might have been made of, or even whether Michelangelo had originally used any at all. We do know that from June to September 1504 the sculptor worked on the scaffoldings around his statue, already set on its pedestal, to finish it. What exactly is meant by "finish it" is uncertain, but in all likelihood the marble was not left without some sort of treatment to close the pores. A particular technique, gold finishing, would deserve special consideration; however, such techniques were usually performed by specialised artisans.

In fact, *David* was not completely white at the time of its unveiling, but must have had a partial gilding, applied as highlighting to "... *la cigna, e 'l broncone e la ghirlanda...*", that is to say the sling, the trunk supporting the right leg and the garland[7]. Finishing of this sort was not out of the ordinary for the time. Renaissance sculptures, like medieval and, even earlier, classical sculptures, were anything but monochrome, and the application of coloured pigments or gold highlighting often completed the surface finish, particularly on the complementary elements, while the human body was preferably left white or unpainted. Rarely, traces of this original appearance of past monuments have remained, significant examples, nearly contemporary to Michelangelo's times, being Donatello's *Annunciation* in Santa Croce and the Forteguerri monument by Verrocchio in the Pistoia Cathedral.

As for the garland, according to payment records of the goldsmith Bastiano di Domenico Cennini, it was made up of twenty-eight leaves of gilded copper. However, whether it encircled the statue's hips or head is still unknown, its function never being better specified. We do however know, as recounted by Pietro Aretino in a letter, that in 1545, the Florentines covered *David's* hips with a gilded garland. The possible hypotheses are therefore the following: either the garland mentioned by Aretino is the original one, and *David* was therefore never entirely naked, or there were two garlands, the original one, placed on the sculpture's head by Michelangelo, and another one added in 1545 to cover the "*pudenda*", as the genitals were then referred to.

Personally, I tend to believe the second hypothesis as more tenable, for a number of reasons. Firstly, it must be considered that the original filigree garland could not have lasted very long, exposed as it was to all manners of risk, and could easily have been destroyed, stolen or lost. But above all, and this is the most compelling argument, the moralistic stance that would have prompted the covering of a naked body is typical of the Counter Reformation. Thus, while it would be difficult to explain such action in 1504, it would correspond well to

the atmosphere reigning almost half a century later, when the Church had already prepared the Council of Trento and Daniele da Volterra chastened the nude figures in Michelangelo's *Universal Judgment* in the Sistine Chapel with comely "knickers".

In any event, whatever David's appearance beforehand, from 1813 on it was protected by a wax layer applied hot. Thus, it was able to hold up until 1842, when Lorenzo Bartolini called the public's attention to the need for greater care and protection of Michelangelo's masterpiece. Unfortunately, the consequences were disastrous: the following year the task of restoration was hastily assigned to the sculptor Aristodemo Costoli, who adopted careless and absolutely deleterious methods, despite the enthusiastic approval garnered from Bartolini himself, intent on judging by the apparent aesthetic results alone, while entirely ignoring the mechanical and chemical effects of the instruments and reagents used. It did not take long for some particularly aware and sensitive Florentines to appreciate the seriousness and extent of the damage that Costoli had caused. In 1852, the Council of the Accademia di Belle Arti, headed by the architect Pasquale Poccianti, was called upon to assess the "dangers that are said to threaten Michelangelo's David". In their final report, they meticulously describe the damage suffered by the sculpture over time and courageously denounce the cleaning methods used in the recent restoration[8].

The first type of damage exhibited by the statue was the evident sulphation, that is, the degeneration of the marble's constituent calcium carbonate into calcium sulphate, commonly called gypsum or chalk, which is water soluble. This chemical reaction, due mainly to the sulphur dioxide in rainwater, causes erosion of sculptures especially in their thinnest parts and those most exposed to the deposition and corrosive actions of water, in the case of *David*, the horizontal surfaces of the head and shoulders, and the rock on which his feet rest. The second type of damage consisted of crackling, which is the formation of many fine small cracks (often seen in chinaware), two areas of which can be seen on David: one behind the trunk over the right leg and a barely perceptible one on the left leg. The third and last type of damage found was directly attributable to the cleansing performed by Aristodemo Costoli, who not only used solvents with up to 50% concentrations of hydrochloric acid, but even sharp metal instruments where the grime was hardest to remove.

The text by Poccianti is a rich source of interesting information in many respects. Firstly, it furnishes precious insights into *David's* history, especially with regard to defining the criteria to follow in future restoration operations. It also provides confirmation that such aggressive cleansing methods were universally approved of in order satisfy the demand for an as white a surface as

Preceding page:
Donatello *Annunciation*, ca 1435, Florence, Church of Santa Croce

Verrocchio, *Forteguerri Monument*, 1481-1489, Pistoia, Cathedral

Following page:
Detail of the top of *David'* head

Detail of the top of his shoulders

Detail of the tree trunk behind his right leg

Detail of his left ankle

Detail of the pedestal area and feet

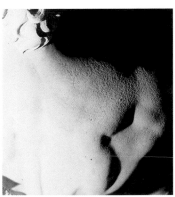

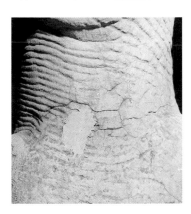

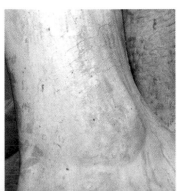

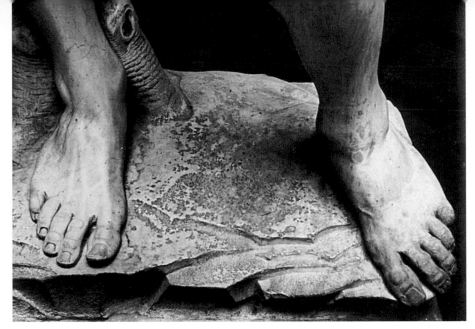

possible, thus giving in to purely subjective taste; not the least consideration was afforded to any aspects of preservation. Unfortunately, it seems that this method became ever more wide-spread, and the condition in which many art-works have reached us (I refer as well to the numerous paintings persistently washed with the highly caustic sodium hydroxide) underscores that the alarm sounded over David was quite justified. In reality, it must be admitted that only recently has the practice of art restoration begun to devote the necessary attention to and respect for age-old patinas and that soft equilibrium of surface shades that Poccianti so wished for a century and a half ago! It must moreover be stressed that removing any and all protective coating from an open-air sculpture signifies leaving it defenceless in the face of atmospheric agents, thereby enormously accelerating its decay.

Thus it appears, not only that Poccianti was right from the very outset of this affair, but that he puts salt on the wound, so to speak, when, as President of the Accademia di Belle Arti, he writes the letter to enclose with his report to the Minister of Public Works. In it he expressly states that for the sake of "reserve", the whole passage concerning the cleansing of the statue had been removed from the copy sent to the Director of State Waterworks, Roads and Workshops[9]. During his appalling job of restoration, Aristodemo Costoli also had to remake a piece of the small toe of the right foot because it had been lost. But the toe was so poorly executed that had to be done over again in 1851, on which occasion, the middle finger of the right hand, which was in danger of detaching, was also consolidated; the unsteady joint is still noticeable today.

As if this were not enough, in the summer of 1847, a plaster mould was made of *David* in order to cast a replica. This operation, apart from leaving traces of the plaster and other substances (generally oily) used to ease the detachment of the mould's sections from the statue's surface, also worsened another aspect of the statue's state, as revealed in Poccianti's report: its static equilibrium.

As mentioned, the stability of the sculpture on its pedestal had been compromised by the 1512 thunderbolt, but thereafter the situation became increasingly worse: crackles and fissures had appeared at the base of both legs.

Clemente Papi, who had made the mould in 1847, suggested the remedy of wrapping the right leg in a tinned copper sheath, which would form an extension of the small tree trunk on which the foot leans. And not only this! our audacious smelter went even further, suggesting that, if the original marble to which the reinforcing structure was to be bound was not strong enough, it should be replaced with a large piece of new material[10].

Fortunately, this project was never carried out, thanks once again to the forceful intervention of Poccianti, who throughout the entire tangled, unedifying affair, seemed to have been the most knowledgeable, trustworthy participant. In 1872 De Fabris, still uncertain of *David*'s stability, suggested that once the statue had been placed in the centre of the Tribune that he had designed, it could be secured by means of a metal tension rod fixed to the back wall[11].

Two more committees were established, one in 1866 and the other in 1871, to oversee the state of maintenance of *David* and assess the proposals for preventing it from deteriorating any further. In the ultimate analysis, it seems that all these committees, and all the discussions by illustrious professors and ex-

Detail of the sling

Detail of the small toe of the right foot

perts during the 19th century only served to inflict more damage on the statue, which they then hastened to try and repair, ineptly causing more damage, which they then hastened to try and repair… This vicious cycle was finally interrupted, at least from the point of view of the statue's maintenance, by the placing of *David* in the Accademia.

On September 14th 1991, *David* was stricken once again, this time not by the hand of God, but by that of a lunatic, Pietro Cannata, who entered the Gallery with a hammer hidden under his jacket, drew near to the statue and with a rapid motion struck its left foot. The tip of the second toe shattered into a thousand fragments, some of which were recovered and used to reconstruct it with the help of acrylic resin and marble powder. Actually, the damage done was quite limited (less than a cubic centimetre of material), but the indignation echoed the world over was immense. There was talk of shutting *David* off within a protective glass case. Debates followed on the dangers to which art works were exposed even in the most secure museums. Finally, a reasonable decision was made: to set up barriers around all of Michelangelo's works in order to keep people at a 'safe' distance, while at the same time not interfere with viewing the sculptures. The good results obtained thereby cannot be denied, on the one hand, because such control is quite easy to manage and, on the other, because it has put a stop to the continuous fingering of the statues' prominent parts, a habit that had produced noticeable accumulations of oily substances on the tip of David's left foot and the knees of the *Prisoners*.

As for total, absolute security, this idea has remained what it is, utopian: a goal incompatible with the demands of real life, even for artworks.

Detail of the right hand

Detail of the marble surface

"... I would consider myself negligent in my duty as an artist and member of the Deputation, if I did not take advantage of the opportunity now granted me to say some words on a topic of great interest: the preservation of all the sculptural monuments of which Florence is justifiably so proud. I intend to speak of the barbaric system recently introduced to subject our marble statues, sculptural groups, busts and bas-reliefs to a sort of washing, so as to restore them to their original whiteness. Nor do I hesitate the least in decrying such a system as barbaric; nor should it be thought that I speak thusly motivated by anything less than due and well-pondered reasons. However, without lingering to underscore the ineptitude of the simple and inexpert hand used in that operation, I believe that I am able to show how such cleansing is not only poorly indicated and short-lived, but also too harmful and ruinous.

And in the first place, it is poorly indicated because it eliminates from our monuments the imprint of their venerable antiquity, and because it deprives them of that indefinable colour by which the spectator's eye experiences a pleasureful quietude in contemplating them. In the second place, it is short-lived because the acidulated liquid that is employed in its execution renders the surface of the marble scabrous, and therefore more liable to accumulate dust and water. In the third place, it is harmful and ruinous because it deprives the limbs and drapings of their richness and softness, and because, as the inauspicious washing is neither uniform, nor single, it corrodes the different parts diversely... I will say, therefore, that all acids, even the less potent ones, such as citric acid, attack the surface of marble, especially the white ones, they penetrate into it, and they corrode it, thusly making it more or less scabrous in its various portions. Now it results from the chemical analysis that the liquid employed in polishing our sculptures contains no less than one half hydrochloric acid, which, as is known, strongly attacks

the carbonate limestones, and therefore in the space of a short time is capable, not of only removing the surface coloured by time, but of penetrating into it, calcining it and dissolving it to the depth of two thousandths of an arm's length. But as the corrosive power of this liquid does not always produce the effect with the desired haste, it is concentrated even further and applied a number of times on the more heavily stained parts, from which it follows that these parts result more highly decayed and consumed. The desolating certainty therefore exists that, by continuing and repeating the ruinous washing, our sculptures will soon present a pathetic spectacle. Nor is this all, given that the destructive actions of the acid are often supplemented by prompter, more effective measures. And I must as well denounce that in the parts more refractory to reacquiring their lost whiteness with the desired haste, as are those most directly exposed to the elements, and in general the cavities in which water and dust collect more easily, no aversion is demonstrated to using sharp instruments.

Nor would I dare to speak in this manner had I not encountered lesions in the David himself.

This then is the price paid for the fatuous pleasure of restoring our monuments to the whiteness of quarry marble!"

(Florence, Archives of the Accademia di Belle Arti, file 41 A, 98, year 1852)

David and his place: building the Tribune and planning a Michelangelo Museum

The fact that *David* had finally been sheltered from the elements unfortunately did not put an immediate end to the adversities it had to face. As if in a tragicomedy, the statue, recently set on its new pedestal (the original one was destroyed during the move), was shut inside a giant wooden crate and abandoned in the middle of nowhere, because in 1873 the Tribune had been planned, but not yet built.

The situation that year was the following. De Fabris had initially planned a square architectural space at the end of what had until then been called the painting gallery (which now corresponds to the hall of the Prisoners or Slaves) because its walls were hung with paintings from the 14th century, as can be seen in a painting by Odoardo Borrani now in the National Gallery of Modern Art in Rome. It was immediately clear that it would be extremely convenient to create a connection between this gallery and the other great hall of the Accademia di Belle Arti, which stretched parallel to it, the sculpture gallery (today the 19th-century room). At the time, the two areas were in fact not connected, each having a separate entrance in Via del Cocomero, now Via Ricasoli.

Because of the substantial modifications needed, as well as the normally slow bureaucratic process, when *David* was removed from Piazza della Signoria not even the walls of the Tribune had been built yet, let alone the planned skylight. Thus, the statue had to be stored inside a wooden hut in the countryside. In November, with the first rains, some stains formed on the surface of the marble. Once again a committee was hastily formed and, after having made their survey, decreed that there was nothing to fear, because the stains in question were only mould and with the coming of the warm season everything would return as before[12]. Apparently,

Odoardo Borrani, *The Gallery of the Accademia in Florence* (ca 1860), National Gallery of Modern Art, Rome

Florence, Gallery of the Accademia, view of the 19th-century room

no one was overly concerned about the damage consequent to simply sequestering Michelangelo's masterpiece from public view and leaving Piazza della Signoria bare.

In the meantime, celebrations were being planned for the five-hundredth anniversary of Michelangelo's birth, and the walls under construction were decorated with cloth curtains and make-shift displays, while the idea was taking form of creating a Michelangelo museum centred round *David*. Actually, the first concrete proposal for such an institution regarded Casa Buonarroti and had been formulated many years prior by the numismatologist and art collector Marco Guastalla[13]. The anniversary of 1875, together with the concomitance of the ongoing work for *David's* placement, brought the idea back into the limelight, this time with stronger arguments and a more suitable place, the Accademia di Belle Arti. The intention was to assemble the greatest possible number of plaster casts of works in Italy and abroad, as well as all types of documentation (sketches, photographs, manuscripts) in order to illustrate the life and work of Michelangelo. The educational intent of the museum was explicit and in keeping with new trends in the field of museology arising primarily in the Anglo-Saxon world. However, a second aim was to enrich the museum's holdings with original works. Thus, after *St. Mathew* was transferred to the Accademia in 1831, it was requested, in vain, that the *Prisoners* be moved there from the Grotto of Buontalenti in Boboli Gardens, where they were quickly deteriorating. Instead, a cast of *Moses* was acquired, together with those of *Rachel* and *Leah* from San Pietro in Vincoli, the *Risen Christ* from Santa Maria sopra Minerva in Rome, and the bust of *Pope Paul III* from the Capodimonte Museum. Many other casts followed: the town hall of Rome donated one of the Vatican *Pietà* and the *Rondanini Pietà*; copies of *The candelabrum angel and St. Petronius* from the Arca (Shrine) di San Domenico arrived from Bologna; the Linguistic Academy of Genoa supplied a bas-relief thought to have been done by Michelangelo. From abroad came a cast of the *Madonna of Bruges*, one of the *Prisoners* in the Louvre and the *Squatting Youth* from the Hermitage, while the *Taddei Tondo* was represented by an incision. The Accademia in Florence was already in possession of casts of the *Medici Tombs* from the New Sacristy of San Lorenzo, so its holdings now represented an impressive cross section of Michelangelo's lifework.

However, the available space hardly seemed sufficient for the new collection, and De Fabris accordingly modified his design in mid-construction. The original idea of a square layout was changed to a broad Greek cross with two side wings and one longitudinal one, at whose centre *David* would be set. Then, for reasons of space, one wing had to be made longer than the other, as we can see today.

34

Placing of the copy of David in Piazza della Signoria, 1910, Flornce, Photo Archives of the Museum "Firenze com'era"

Once the anniversary celebrations were over, progress slowed and the Gallery was finally inaugurated on July 22nd 1882, amidst a great deal of controversy. Disputes arose mainly over the many horizontal and vertical *pietra serena* friezes along the wall and on the dome behind *David*, and especially the cornice which "running along the niche before which David stands passes cruelly through the line of the statue's neck, interrupting its serene and harmonious form"[14]. Today this unpleasant effect is no longer noticeable because, at some undetermined time since then, all the stone profiling on the back of the Tribune, including the fateful cornice, were completely painted over the some same colour as the masonry walls, so that for better or worse, all traces of the original decorative design have been eliminated. Nevertheless, it seems that the presence of such a prominent mesh of grey lines, on the one hand, would make reading the work more difficult by confusing its profile, and on the other, restrict the space around the statue, which is already narrow, at least in comparison to its original setting outdoors. The best idea in De Fabris' design was undoubtedly the skylight, which has left

The Tribune of the Gallery of the Accademia in Florence, between 1903 and 1909, AFSPMF (Photo Archives of the Florentine Museums's Superintendency)

Opposite:
The Tribune for *David* at the Gallery of the Accademia in Florence, between 1884-1900, Fratelli Alinari Photo Archive, photo by Brogi

David some link, albeit a limited one, with the atmosphere and shades of natural lighting, waxing and waning with the passing hours of the day and months of the year, just as when it stood imperiously before Palazzo Vecchio.

In 1882 the new museum was separated from the Accademia di Belle Arti and entrusted to the Royal Galleries. The museum now had its own entry ticket and visiting hours. The business of the Academy was born with the exhibition of *David*. While *David's* fortunes have never faltered since, the fate of the Michelangelo Museum has instead been uncertain and fraught with obstacles, at least in the all-embracing, pedagogical conception that had characterised its origins. The idea of a collection of copies was destined for a frosty reception by a public accustomed to going about their daily affairs amidst world-renowned originals: as experience has by now shown, educational tools can prepare for and supplement direct contact with great art, but they cannot replace it; their function is fundamentally different. Nowadays, this fact is even more evident, as such tools have become far more sophisticated in their ability to stimulate the curiosity and attract ever broader segments of the public, while at the same time offering heretofore unheard of possibilities for faithfully reproducing original works of art. We all know *David*, we have all seen innumerable photographs and reproductions, but how many of us actually believe that such experiences could possibly substitute for crossing that threshold and traversing that hall accompanied by the *Prisoners* up to the feet of *David* himself.

The changes in cultural climate that marked the turn of the century, the new trends in museology towards less historicism and greater aestheticism, favoured a strongly emotional approach to art. Copies, photographs and documents had little by little lost much of their attraction, while the collection of 14th and 15th-century painting, the so-called "Primitives", now on display in the three expressly prepared rooms flanking the Tribune (today called the Florentine rooms) began to attract crowds as never before.

Unexpectedly, after many vain attempts made the enterprise seem hopeless, in 1906 King Vittorio Emanuele III granted authorization to remove the *Prisoners* from Buontalenti's Grotto in Boboli. That same year the academy donated to the Gallery a cast of the *River God* (in storage at Casa Buonarroti since 1965) and then in 1909 *St. Matthew*, which was placed together with the *Prisoners* in the long corridor leading up to *David,* freed by now of all other objects. The Gallery was then inaugurated once again, now in a layout very similar to that for which it has since become famous the world over.

"Florence October 20th 1875

The temporary adornments and the decorations, which afforded a decent appearance to the impromptu Halls in the premises of the Accademia for the exhibition of Michelangelo's works, no longer exist, and the constructions commenced there for the Tribune of the David have re-emerged just as they appeared in the early days of September past, that is, as far as the area where the arches and vaults are to be placed. The proverbial wooden crate that covered the praiseworthy statue has returned to defend it from the elements, but also to obscure it from universal admiration; and the architectural cornices, elegantly cut from pietra serena, lay exposed, to their great detriment, to the rains and the rigours of the cold.

It is to be believed that this state of affairs will not be of long duration; rather, it is to be fervently hoped that it will cease as soon as possible for those many reasons of which each of us is well aware and which I therefore refrain from enumerating [...].

The work, suspended since October of the aforesaid year of 1873, was taken up again at the close of the month of September 1874, following the Decree issued by the special Committee in assembly on the 4th day of the preceding month of July, whereby call was made to recommence the above-ground constructions and advance as far as the allowances left available permitted, that is, up to the sum of Liras 28,018.17. And it is to such dictate that I conform.

Meanwhile, the occasion established to celebrate with solemn honours the IV centenary of Michelangelo drew near, and the committee governing said festivities determined that in the halls of the Accademia, and more especially round the statue of the David, there should be held an exhibition of the most noteworthy sculptures of the great artist, plaster casts of which had been promised by the government, the city hall in Rome, and other diverse institutes and academies of Europe. And

*in truth, this seemed a sound proposition, not only be-
cause extremely fitting on that solemn occasion, but
better still because it gave a solid fundament to the creation of a true Michelangelesque Museum, which centred on the masterpiece of the divine Buonarroti will
bestow lustre and credit upon our city.*

*But such concept, stupendous in itself, has brought
about a new order of ideas with relation to art; in that
it was an easy matter to realise that the tribune con-
ceived of in 1872 with the sole purpose of holding the
statue of the David, would have been insufficient for the
new purpose to which, by virtue of the decreed immi-
nent exposition, was to provide, per force.*

*Therefore, without further ado, given these most accu-
rate considerations on the matter, I could recognise
that without altering or adjusting in any way what has
already been done, it was a simple matter to consider-
ably increase the perimeter of the commenced building,
departing from the foundations that in other times had
been predestined for that place; and precisely on the
right side of the tribune [...] when the thought occurred
under the past Grand-duchy Government to enlarge the
establishment of the Accademia. I realized that by
building on those and exploiting the walls already built
on the left side for the room communicating with the
ancient picture gallery, I would have easily been able to
convert the square of the original tribune into the form
of a Greek cross. And it finally seemed clear to me that
in the three wings or arms of the design, transformed
thusly, I could find the space required to prepare in a
fitting manner, not only the sculptural works that were
being collected for those solemn celebrations, but also
as the others that would be added subsequently to fur-
nish a stable settlement and completion to the envis-
aged Michelangelesque Museum."*

(Florence Municipal Historical Archives, file 5324, insert 10)

Copying David

The idea of copying *David* occurred very early – clearly before the era of bookshops and copyright protection – but even before its removal from Piazza della Signoria created the need for something to replace it. In the summer of 1847, just after the fateful restoration by Aristodemo Costoli, the smelter Clemente Papi made a plaster mould of *David,* composed of more than 1,500 segments, some weighing as much as 680 kg. On August 29th 1846, the grand duke, who intended to have a bronze version cast, had already ordered a mould to be made, but the undertaking was delayed interminably by the exorbitant costs involved. He finally decided to make do with a plaster copy, which would of course remain at his disposal should he need it any time in the future. This operation, coveted by Papi as well, had an unquestionably positive outcome for the maintenance of *David*: since then, there has no longer been any need to make moulds of the original, and even today, when a full-sized replica of *David* is asked for, it can be cast from the 19th-century plaster mould, now kept at the Gipsoteca of the Istituto d'Arte di Porta Romana as part of its plaster cast collection.

Nevertheless, the operation performed in 1847 was not devoid of negative effects on the statue's surface. Firstly, in order to detach the plaster segments with greater ease, before their application the surface of the sculpture was first smeared with fatty or soapy compounds, some rather conspicuous traces of which usually remained, for the most part in the form of superficial deposits. Secondly, as the plaster was compressed forcibly onto the statue in order to achieve perfect adherence and adaptation to the smallest elements of its sculpting, it penetrated irreversibly in the micro-fissures and pores of the marble. Finally, one need only consider the enormous weight of the plaster segments (as much as 680 kg each) to which the sculpture was subjected in order to realise the consequences of that regrettable operation on David's stability.

The bronze replica, deemed too costly in 1846, was eventually cast in 1866 in the wake of the enthusiasm engendered by Italy's unification and the establishment of its capital in Florence. Nevertheless, as much as this bronze David was appreciated (it earned great praise at the Paris International Exposition in 1867), its dark polished metal surface was judged incompatible with the chromatic equilibrium of Piazza della Signoria and therefore unsuitable to filling the void left by the transfer of the original to the Gallery of the Accademia. The bronze was eventually placed in the centre of the square that Giuseppe Poggi created midway in the ring of avenues built along the course of the old city walls, today known as Piazzale Michelangelo. At its feet were placed copies, also bronze, of the allegorical figures on the *Medici Tombs* of the New Sacristy in San Lorenzo, thereby forming a monumental "pastiche" that was immediately the object of fierce and not unfounded criticism. The entire episode ignited an intense, long debate on the issue of art reproductions and their relation to the original works, a debate that was to widen to include the more general theme of the intrinsic reproducibility (or irreproducibility) of the artistic act. At the turn of the 19th century, artists and men of

culture regularly expressed their opinions on such matters in newspapers and magazines (particularly, "Il Marzocco"), testament to how vigilant and critical the Florentines were regarding their city's status as a centre of art and the new problems posed by industrial and technological evolution to the nature and future of art. However, after more than a full century of vexation, many of the questions that arose then are still being asked today, still without any certain replies; some we have simply stopped asking, despite our never having found any answers.

One issue still pertinent today is whether, in the long run, the abuse of an image, in the sense of too great an exposure (as is clearly the case with *David*), does not ruin and obfuscate our understanding of it. That is to say, whether seeing replicas and pictures of *David* all over the place, and entirely out of context, does not keep us from really "seeing" it, unhampered by the thousands of false effigies from which we have created a mental image. Perhaps we no longer even manage to "listen" to it, because we have stripped it of all its power to communicate above the din of the multitude.

And still today we must ask ourselves whether it is right to fill our cities with copies, uncertain whether this will make little difference, or a great difference (perhaps too great). And if this difference were, in any event, inescapable and we must therefore bow our heads to it? Or are there perhaps other paths to follow and other value scales to be considered. We look at the copy of Donatello's

Florence, Piazzale Michelangelo, view of the bronze monument

Judith; we look at the *Porta del Paradiso* (*Gate of Heaven*); and we must eye, doubtfully, what Domenico Trentacoste wrote a century ago: "He who copies is bound to a continuous mechanical task that has nothing to do with the living, free force of the creative artist. These – and Michelangelo was one *par excellence* – draw their creations directly from the block, zealously working to grasp the various aspects of life and things, and thereby create beauty. Those who copy, instead, timidly attempt to reproduce the external features that are the final result of a profound, mysterious spiritual act, in whose emotion they do not participate in the least. Such is their state of mind and the conditions of their work, which must necessarily reflect on the result and produce, between the original and the copy, those tangible differences that can hardly be expressed in words, but that the practiced eye discovers at once. Small differences? As great as those separating life from death."[15]

It was in this heated atmosphere that Luigi Arrighetti was to perform the marble replica that would eventually replace the original in Piazza della Signoria in 1910.

Lorenzo Ghiberti and assistants, *Gate of Heaven,* 1425-1452, Florence, Museum of the Opera di Santa Maria del Fiore

Copy of the *Gate of Heaven*, 1990, Florence, Baptistry of San Giovanni

David and Renaissance Florence

From 1501 to 1504 Michelangelo took on the challenge of this work, which the Florentine's would from the outset dub the "Colossus". David is in fact the first modern larger than life statue. Its dimensions can be explained, rather banally, by the fact that the position originally planned for it was, as already mentioned, very high up on the façade of Palazzo Vecchio, which would have cancelled out the colossus effect. What is more, it was supposed to represent the crowning piece of a monumental architectural complex. However, the subsequent decision to set it on the grounds of the square, despite its extraordinary dimensions, involved a deliberate choice and serves to underscore the conceptual difference between Michelangelo's David and Donatello's, while at the same time, demarcating the boundaries between the early Florentine Humanist movement and the Renaissance.

The biblical character David appears numerous times in the 15th-century Floren-

Donatello, *David*, 1408, Florence, Bargello National Museum

Verrocchio, *David*, ca 1465, Florence, Bargello National Museum

tine figurative tradition. The story of the young boy who, completely naked and armed only with a sling and stones, advances dauntlessly against the gargantuan Goliath and succeeds in defeating him by striking him full in the forehead was invested with particular symbolism. David is armed with an invisible, but powerful weapon: faith in his convictions. It is his force of spirit that enables him, unhesitatingly, to overcome the overwhelming brute physical force of the dread enemy. David is the incarnation of Florence during the time of Lorenzo il Magnifico, a city made powerful, not by virtue of arms or wealth, but by superior intelligence and culture. David is Lorenzo il Magnifico, who holds the balance of power in Italy, who win wars through the astuteness of diplomacy, art and poetry. David is Machiavelli, who, armed with the sharp acumen of his intellect, blow by blow, cuts a new path to the understanding of history and politics. For Florentine humanism, the god of David is not the god of the Bible, though he is just as beloved: it is faith in man's ability to dominate the universe through Reason. In the figurative arts, the instrument *par excellence* and the insignia of such power is perspective, whose rules serve to measure the world view, thereby rationalising it. It is this inner strength that leads Florence to victory against its enemies, like frail David against the Goliath.

But Michelangelo's David is not frail. Donatello's is: he has the slender legs,

Ottaviano Vannini, *Lorenzo il Magnifico among the artists*, 1635-1642, Florence, Silverworks Museum, Room of Giovanni da San Giovanni

Following pages (beside Michelangelo's *David*):
Donatello, *David*, 1440-1450, Florence, Bargello National Museum

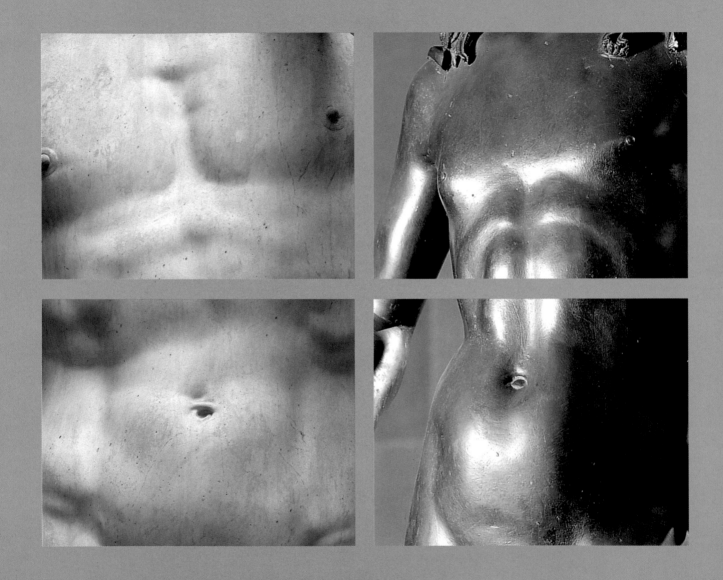

fleshy hips and yet-to-broadened chest of a young boy; the helmet and the large sword seem out of place – far too heavy for his slight frame. This image corresponds to the biblical account, but not Michelangelo's. Michelangelo instead proffers the image of an idealised man of absolute aesthetic perfection, portrayed in the prime of his youthful manhood.

The model that Michelangelo has in mind is classical sculpture, while Donatello is instead thinking of a boy, any boy off the streets of Florence, because Donatello and those of his time still believed that a Florentine boy could transform history, be the hero of a myth. The ideal could be embodied in real life, as perhaps Michelangelo himself also believed while strolling through the "Gardens of San Marco" scrutinising age-old sculptures and discussing philosophy. But at the start of the 16ᵗʰ century, after ten years of bloodshed, after having seen death take Lorenzo il Magnifico, culture reduced to ashes in Savonarola's pyres, foreigners enter the city as its masters and the Cathedral of Santa Maria del Fiore desecrated by an assassin how then did Michelangelo conceive of his art? So, while Botticelli seemed deluged by a cyclone that dishevels the hair even of his Madonnas, no longer the sweet creatures they once were, through his *David* Michelangelo tells us that the ideal is hidden within the marble, and man can only strive to chisel it out in order to allow us to admire it from afar, something which no longer belongs to us.

One question often posed regarding Michelangelo's *David* is whether the hero is depicted before or after combat, given the fact that Goliath's disembodied head is missing, as is his sword in the hands of the victor. In the foregoing perspective, this question loses all meaning, or rather, must be framed in different terms. What we see, is not in fact David, the biblical character, defined through his characteristic attributes, but a meta-historical *exemplum*, a symbol of the heroism and excellence which the whole of humanity, not the individ-

53

ual, can attain. Viewed in this perspective, the iconographic details do not matter, but only what David represents. After all, in a certain sense, it is as if this sculpture were one more example of Michelangelo's technique of *non finito*, works that he purposely left "not finished" in either their iconographic or formal aspects. The unfinished quality of many of his works can often be explained by a number of incidental circumstances, such as, in the case of the *Prisoners,* the constant changes in the design of the tomb dictated by Pope Julius II della Rovere, and in the case of *David,* the fact that Michelangelo had to work a marble block already partially sculpted by others. However, above and beyond these rather banal influences, other deeper, more pondered motivations cannot be ignored. Michelangelo sets forth his conception of the artistic act a number of times in his writings, some in verse: "*Non ha l'ottimo artista alcun concetto \ ch'un marmo solo in sé non circoscriva \ col suo soverchio, e solo a quello arriva \ la man che ubbidisce all'intelletto*" (The great artist has no concept \ what a marble may have confined \ within it depths; that can be divined \ only by the hand subject to the intellect). Which means that the formal or iconographic definition is pursued up to the point in which the hand manages, through the work of chiselling, to bring forth (and therefore make evident to the world) the idea already existing there, eternally, beyond the phenomenological.

Prisoners, Young Slave, ca 1530, Florence, Gallery of the Accademia

Prisoners, Reawakening Slave, ca 1530, Florence, Gallery of the Accademia

Prisoners, Bearded Slave, ca 1530, Florence, Gallery of the Accademia

David today

And today, what is *David* today? What does it stand for?

Nowadays some 1.2 million peoplea year come to see *David*, spending on the average half an hour in the Gallery of the Accademia. Although this is an entirely subjective estimate, I believe that the first-floor rooms, which are wholly removed from the path through Michelangelo's work, is visited by no more than 10% of all those who enter. Instead, the 19th-century room, where the plasters by Lorenzo Bartolini and Luigi Pampaloni are on exhibit, attracts a great deal of visitors, mostly (and unfortunately) because it opens onto the Tribune, and many enter hoping to find other works by Michelangelo. In fact, even on exiting many believe that they have seen two or three hundred works by Michelangelo! Some dubious ones have asked me if that were so, and I have always replied no. I do not know why I have disillusioned so many tourists that way – excessive love of truth, I guess. Sometimes the visit is very, very hasty, even as little as fifteen minutes to enter, buy tickets, get through the Tribune, stop beneath *David* and run off. On one of my first days at the Accademia, back in 1981, I saw a group head for the exit exactly 12 minutes after the Museum's opening. I thought that they had taken a wrong turn and was about to stop them, when I, in turn, was stopped by a custodian who explained to me that they were leaving because they had "already done it all"!

Sometimes the visit is very, very unknowing. A few years ago, a series of interviews was performed of the people waiting in the long queue before the Accademia in Via Ricasoli, in which they were asked if they knew what they were going to see. The replies ran the full gamut, from "Michelangelo's house" to "something by Michelangelo". In any event, as it turned out, a great number of people were waiting for hours under the sun without knowing exactly why…

So*, David* is a myth.

Myths are not to be understood; we must not ask questions of them. They serve to let ourselves be transported outside reality; as in an act of faith. And *David*, in its well-chosen position in the centre of a cross, underscores the ambiguous contamination between the sacred and the profane, an aspect which right from the outset Michelangelo himself strived for, imparting to a biblical character the appearance and pose typical of a triumphant hero of classical Greek sculpture, so much so that the Florentine Signoria had it removed from the Cathedral and placed in a public place.

But David is not always a myth sought after only to satisfy an inner need: it is often an imposed myth: seeing it is nearly a social obligation, a pilgrimage to the Mecca of the western world. This of course fills the coffers, but it also strips the work of its cultural value and, in the long run, risks demeaning it. Soon it will be the five hundredth anniversary of *David's* creation, and our programme for such an exceptional occasion aims at restoring a profound, truly universal significance to this age-old myth.

Following page:
Protection for Michelangelo's *David* and *Prisoners* in the Gallery of the Accademia during the Second World War

Notes

[1] G. Gaye, *Documenti di Storia Italiana, Carteggio inedito di artisti,* 3 voll., Florence 1839-1840, vol. II [1840], p. 464. Gaye draws his text from *Diario fiorentino* by Luca Landucci.

[2] F. Vossilla, *La Loggia dei Lanzi,* Florence 1995, p. 137.

[3] Manetti's letter is published in A. Gotti, *Vita di Michelangelo,* Florence 1875, vol. II, appendix 5, pp. 37-39.

[4] G. Gaye, *Documenti di Storia Italiana,* cit., vol. II [1840], p. 458.

[5] J. Nardi, *Istorie della città di Firenze,* Florence 1838-1841, vol. I [1838], book V, p. 456.

[6] Florence, Library of the Uffizi Gallery, ms. n. 277

[7] With regard to the gilding and the question of the garland, see R. Weil Garris, *On the pedestals of Michelangelo's David, Bandinelli's Ercules and Cacus and the sculpture of Piazza della Signoria*, in "Römisches Jahrbuch für Kunstgeschichte", 1983, pp. 377-415 [p.385] and R. Ristori, *L'Aretino, il David di Michelangelo e la "modestia fiorentina"*, in "Rinascimento", second series, XXVI, 1986, p. 77-97.

[8] Florence, Archives of the Accademia di Belle Arti, file 41 A, n.98, year 1852.

[9] Florence, Archives of the Accademia di belle Arti, file 41 A, n. 98.

[10] Florence, Archives of the Accademia di Belle Arti, file 41 A, n. 98, year 1852.

[11] Florence Municipal Historical Archives, special file 5324, ins. 4.

[12] Florence, Archives of the Accademia di Belle Arti, file 62, 30, year 1873, ins. 30.

[13] Florence, Moderno Buonarroti Archive, Box B, ins. 42, year 1863.

[14] *La tribuna Michelangiolesca*, in "Arte e storia", vol. I, 1883, p. 67.

[15] D. Trentacoste, *La copia del David. I dubbi di uno scultore,* in "Il Marzocco" IX, April 24, 1904.

An itinerary through Michelangelo's works in Florence

Gallery of the Accademia

David
Four *Prisoners (*or *Slaves)* for the Tomb of Pope Julius II della Rovere.
St. Matthew, one of the twelve Apostles commissioned from Michelangelo for the pillars of the Florentine Cathedral.
The *Palestrina Pietà*, the marble group discovered in 1939 in the Barberini Chapel in Palestrina, near Rome; today considered by most scholars not to be by Michelangelo.

Casa Buonarroti Museum

Battle of the Centaurs and *Madonna of the Stairs*, marble bas-reliefs performed early in his career, while a guest at the court of Lorenzo il Magnifico.
River God, a model made of clay, wood, straw and various other materials, perhaps as part of the decorations for the New Sacristy at San Lorenzo.
Numerous terracotta and wax models, sketches and writings.
Documentation on the artist's life and work.

Monument complex of San Lorenzo

Medici Tombs in the New Sacristy of the Basilica.
Medici Library: design of the staircase and the wooden high-backed chairs.

Museo dell'Opera di Santa Maria del Fiore (Cathedral Works Museum)

Pietà, marble group for his own tomb.

Bargello National Museum

Bacchus, executed in Rome for Cardinal Raffaele Riario and then purchased by his friend and patron, Jacopo Galli.

David-Apollo, perhaps executed as part of the work for the New Sacristy in San Lorenzo.

Bust of Brutus.

Gallery of the Uffizi

Doni Tondo, painting on wood panel depicting the *Holy family with Young St. John the Baptist*, commissioned by Agnolo Doni.

Palazzo Vecchio, Salone dei Cinquecento (Hall of the Five hundred)

Victory, sculpture group originally destined for the tomb of Pope Julius II della Rovere.

Basilica of Santo Spirito

Wooden *Crucifix*, early work sculpted for the monastery where Michelangelo had a room.

Palazzo Medici Riccardi

Two "*finestre inginocchiate*", that is, "kneeling windows", whose stone side frames curve downwards until they rest on the ground.

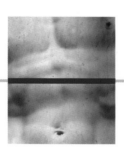

printed in July 2009
by Media Print - Livorno

for
s i l l a b e